SCIENCE CORNER

Popcorn

Light and Dark

Angela Royston

Explore the world with **Popcorn** - your complete first non-fiction library.

Look out for more titles in the **Popcorn** range. All books have the same format of simple text and vibrant images. Text is carefully matched to the pictures to help readers to identify and understand key vocabulary.
www.waylandbooks.co.uk/popcorn

First published in 2010 by Wayland
Copyright © Wayland 2010

This paperback edition published in 2010
by Wayland
Reprinted in 2011

Wayland
338 Euston Road
London NW1 3BH

Wayland Australia
Level 17/207 Kent Street
Sydney NSW 2000

Editor: Katie Powell
Designer: Robert Walster
Picture Researcher: Diana Morris

British Library Cataloguing in Publication Data
Royston, Angela.
   Light and dark. -- (Popcorn. Science corner)
   1. Light--Juvenile literature.
   I. Title II. Series
   535-dc22
ISBN: 978 0 7502 6439 6

Printed and bound in China

Wayland is a division of Hachette Children's Books,
an Hachette UK Company.
www.hachette.co.uk

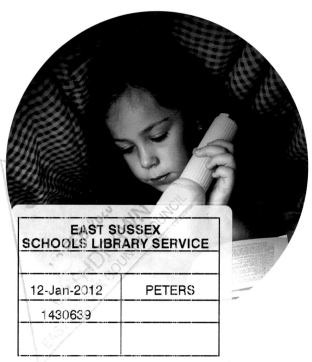

Photographs:
Amskad/Shutterstock: 16.
Atanasidk/Shutterstock: 10. AVTG/istockphoto:
8. Carmen Martinez Banus/istockphoto: front
cover, 2, 12. Mike Bentley/istockphoto: 17.
Thomas Frey/Imagebroker/Alamy: 19.
Don Gray/Photofusion/Alamy: 18. Tony
Hallas/Science Faction/Corbis: 9.
Kokoju/Shutterstock: 1, 4. Slobo
Mitii/istockphoto: 20. S Greg
Panosian/istockphoto: 5. Parema/istockphoto:
11. Robert Pernell/istockphoto: 15. Photogenes:
7. Chris Scredon/istockphoto: 21. Peter
Viisiman/istockphoto: 13. Wayland: 22, 23.
Serdar Yagii/istockphoto: 14.
Peter Zelei/istockphoto: 6.x

Contents

What is light and dark?

Light allows us to see. We can only see something when there is a light shining on it.

A spotlight picks out the dancer on the stage.

Seeing is one of our five senses. The other senses are hearing, smelling, tasting and touching.

If there is no light, it is dark and we cannot see. To be able to see in the dark, we need to use lights.

Street lamps light the way across this bridge at night.

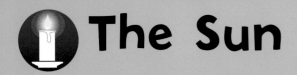 The Sun

During the day we get light from the Sun.
Daylight is brightest on a sunny day.

Do not look at the Sun. Its light is so strong it can hurt your eyes.

The light from the Sun is so strong that
it even shines through clouds and rain.

Night-time

In the evening the Sun sets. It goes out of sight and we can no longer see its light. The sky becomes darker, and then it is night.

Sometimes the clouds look red as the Sun sets.

At night you can see the lights of the stars. We only get a little bit of light from the stars because they are so far away.

A shooting star shines for a few seconds and then it disappears.

Seeing in the dark

At night people usually turn on electric lights so that they can see. Electric lights use electricity to make light.

At night millions of lights in buildings and on the streets light up the city.

People use different kinds of light to help them to see in the dark. Something that makes light is called a source of light.

This electric lamp makes it easier for this man to read his book.

Other sources of light

At night people use a variety of different sources of light. A torch is useful because it is easy to hold and carry around.

A torch lights up a small area at a time.

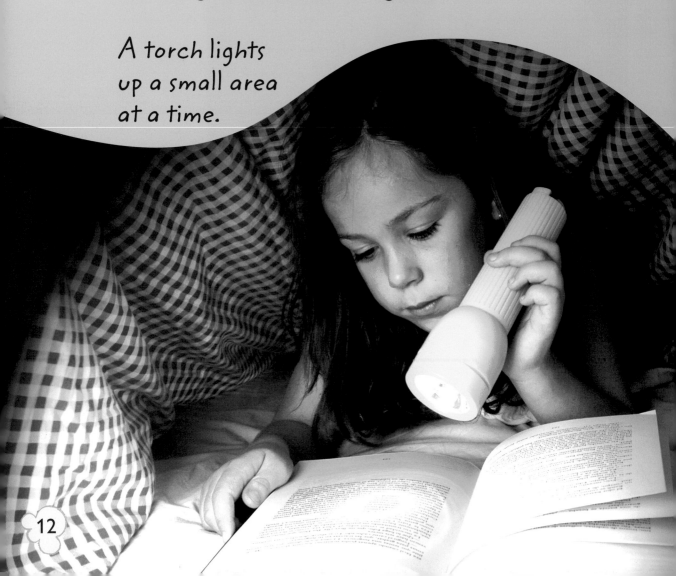

Cars and other vehicles have headlamps. The drivers turn them on at night. They help the drivers to see the road ahead.

Headlamps help other people to see the vehicle at night, too.

Shiny objects

Things made of metal or glass sometimes shine with light. This is called a reflection. Some objects reflect light from another light source.

The glass windows of this building are reflecting light from the Sun.

Things that are smooth and shiny reflect light well. Some bicycles have a special reflector that reflects light.

Small prisms inside the reflector reflect light.

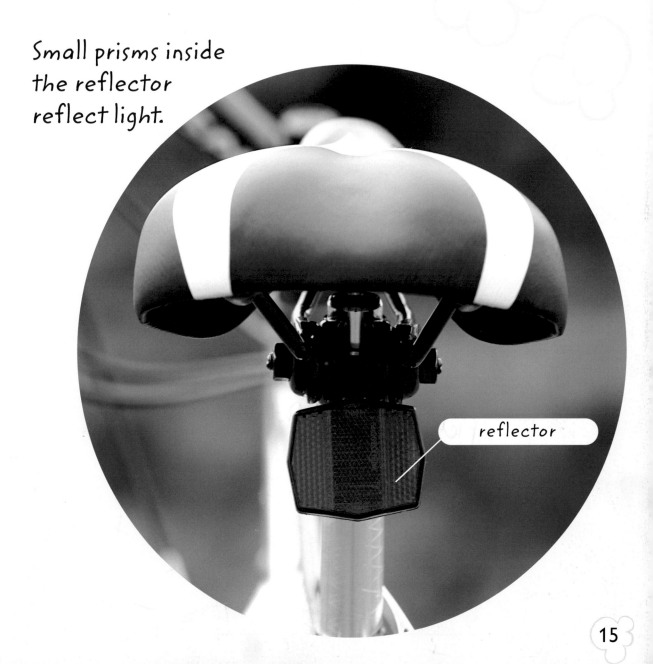

reflector

Things that sparkle

Some things sparkle when they reflect light. Sequins are small metal discs that are sewn onto clothes.

These sequins reflect sunlight when the dancers move.

Tinsel can be used to decorate Christmas trees. Tinsel is made of short strands of metal. The metal reflects light.

Safety patches

Some coats and shoes have shiny patches.
The patches reflect light at night.

People who cycle at night should always wear reflecting safety patches.

Patches that reflect light help to keep
you safe in the dark. The light from car
headlamps reflects off the patches. This
helps drivers and other people to see you.

Warning lights

Lights are also used to warn you of danger. Fire engines have flashing lights so that you can see them coming.

This fire engine's bright lights and loud siren help you to see and hear where it is.

This red light tells you not to cross
the road. You must wait for the
green light.

What should you do to cross the road safely at traffic lights?

Does it sparkle?

Find out which of these objects sparkle in the light.

1. Here are some objects. Find out which sparkle and which don't.

2. Hold the paperclip up to the torch. Does it sparkle?

22

3. Now try holding the pencil up to the torch light. Does it sparkle?

4. Finally, do the same with the tinsel.

5. Make a chart to show which objects sparkled and which did not.

23

Glossary

electricity a form of energy that is used to make electric machines work

glass a hard material that is easy to break. Windows are made of glass

headlamps two lights on the front of a vehicle

light source where light comes from

metal a hard, shiny material. Saucepans are made of metal

prisms objects that reflect light

reflect the way light hits and bounces off objects

reflection when light hits a surface some of the light bounces off

reflector something that reflects light

senses the ways of knowing what is happening outside and inside your body

stars tiny dots of light that you can see in the sky on a clear night

Index